Triceratops

by Charles Lennie

ABDO
DINOSAURS
Kids

www.abdopublishing.com

Published by Abdo Kids, a division of ABDO, PO Box 398166, Minneapolis, Minnesota 55439.

Copyright © 2015 by Abdo Consulting Group, Inc. International copyrights reserved in all countries. No part of this book may be reproduced in any form without written permission from the publisher.

Printed in the United States of America, North Mankato, Minnesota.

052014

092014

THIS BOOK CONTAINS
RECYCLED MATERIALS

Photo Credits: AP Images, Getty Images, Minnesota Zoo (mnzoo.org), Shutterstock, Thinkstock, ©User:FunkMonk/CC-BY-2.0 p.15, ©Zachi Evenor/CC-BY-2.0 p.21, ©Michael Gray/CC-BY-SA-2.0 p.21

Production Contributors: Teddy Borth, Jennie Forsberg, Grace Hansen

Design Contributors: Candice Keimig, Laura Rask, Dorothy Toth

Library of Congress Control Number: 2013952075

Cataloging-in-Publication Data

Lennie, Charles.

 Triceratops / Charles Lennie.

   p. cm. -- (Dinosaurs)

ISBN 978-1-62970-025-0 (lib. bdg.)

Includes bibliographical references and index.

1. Triceratops--Juvenile literature.   I. Title.

567.915--dc23

                    2013952075

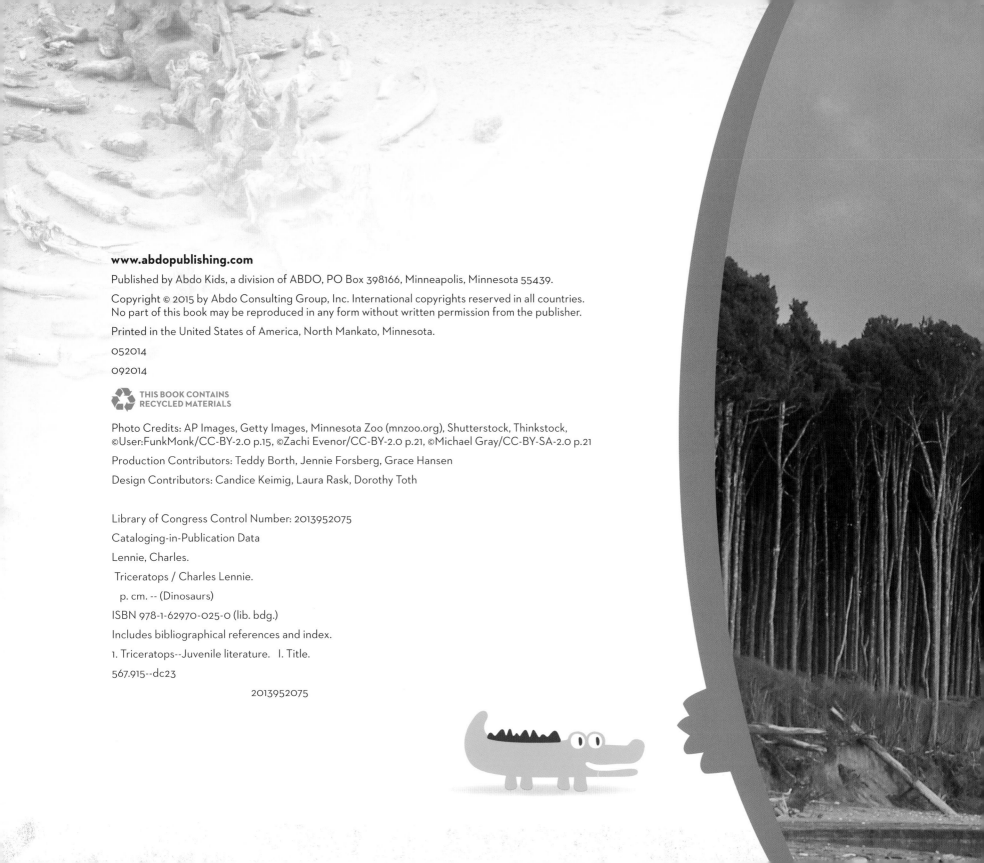

Table of Contents

Triceratops

The Triceratops lived
a long time ago. It lived
about 65 million years ago.

The Triceratops is known for its three horns. It had two long horns and one short horn.

7

The Triceratops' horns grew up to three feet (1 m) long. It used its horns to **protect** itself.

9

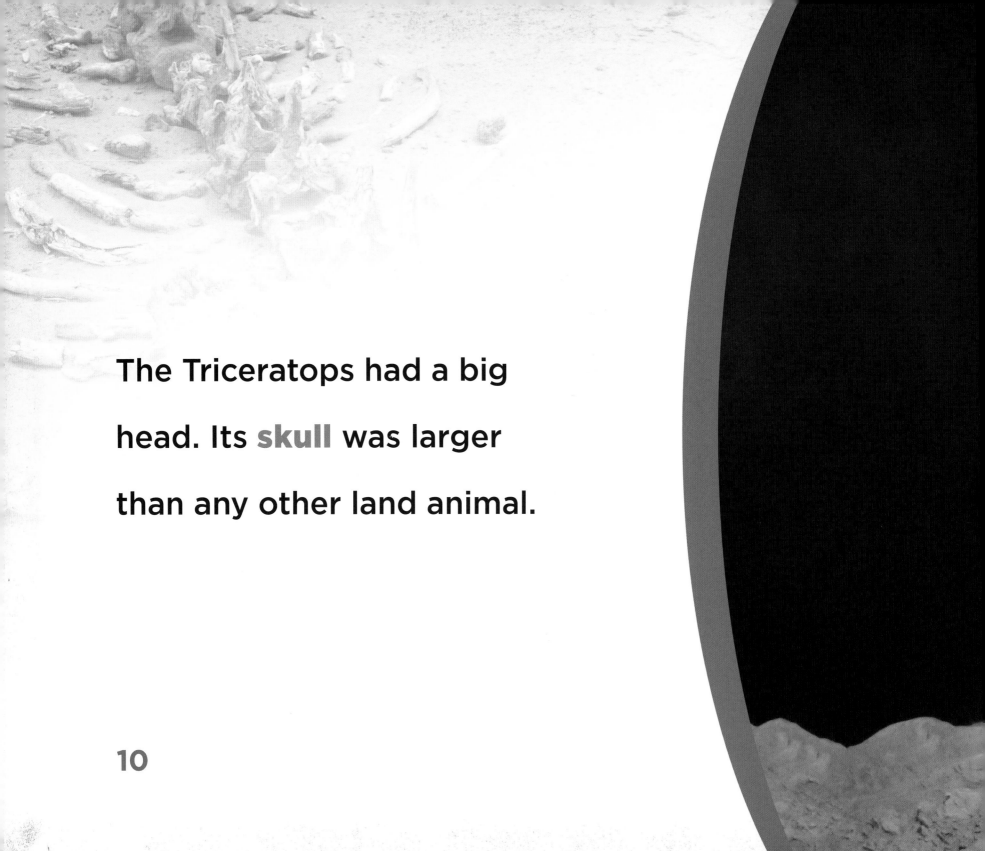

The Triceratops had a big head. Its **skull** was larger than any other land animal.

11

The Triceratops had a **neck frill**.

The frill probably kept its head

and neck safe.

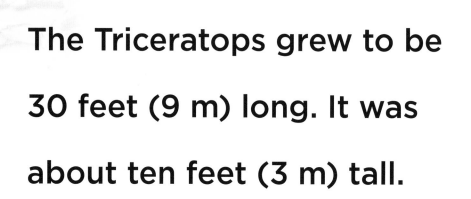

The Triceratops grew to be 30 feet (9 m) long. It was about ten feet (3 m) tall.

The Triceratops had a **beak**.

The beak tore plants.

Food

The Triceratops only ate plants. It had between 400 and 800 teeth.

Fossils

Triceratops **fossils** have been found throughout North America.

Canada

Montana

North Dakota

South Dakota

Wyoming

Colorado

21

More Facts

- The **skull** of a Triceratops was huge. It could grow to be 6 to 10 feet (2 to 3 m) in length!

- An adult Triceratops was about the same size as an adult elephant.

- The word *Triceratops* means "three horned face."

- From 2000 to 2010, over 40 Triceratops skulls were found in Montana, North Dakota, and South Dakota.

Glossary

beak – a hard mouthpart that sticks out.

fossils – the remains of a once living thing; could be a footprint or skeleton.

neck frill – the large, bony plate on the back of a Triceratops' head.

protect – to keep safe.

skull – a bone structure that surrounds your brain and supports your face.

23

Index

abdokids.com

Use this code to log on to abdokids.com and access crafts, games, videos and more!

Abdo Kids Code:
DTK0250